IMF GOLD SALES IN PERSPECTIVE

**Vice Chairman Jim Saxton (R-NJ)
Joint Economic Committee
United States Congress
August 1999**

All rights reserved. No part of this publication
may be reproduced, stored in a retrieval system,
or transmitted in any form or by any means,
electronic, mechanical, photocopying or
otherwise, without the prior permission of the
copyright owner.

For information regarding special discounts for
bulk purchases,
please contact BN Publishing at
info@bnpublishing.net

©Copyright 2009 – BN Publishing
www.bnpublishing.net

ALL RIGHTS RESERVED
Printed in the U.S.A.

Executive Summary

There have been a number of recent calls for the International Monetary Fund (IMF) to sell part of its 103 million ounce gold holdings as part of a plan for debt relief for the heavily indebted poor countries (HIPC). One such proposal has been advanced by the Administration, and officials of several other nations as well as the IMF have voiced support for similar plans. The proposed gold sales would require Congressional approval, and debate on this change in policy is already underway.

Although the exact form of the proposal is not yet clear, there are several reasons for Congress to critically examine this proposal and review the potential for negative consequences:

- The proposal is not transparent in that its content and full ramifications are unclear, and it may ultimately facilitate financing for certain IMF operations without conventional authorization and oversight.
- The proposed gold sales would tap a hidden IMF gold reserve that can be viewed as belonging to member countries.

The cost of the proposal to the U.S. would amount to half a billion dollars, relative to restitution to member countries.

- Continued gold sales may weaken the IMF's balance sheet. With one-third of its outstanding credits from its main account owed by Russia and Indonesia, it is reasonable to question whether potential weakening of the IMF's financial position is desirable at this time. The money contributed by the taxpayers of the U.S. and other nations is exposed in IMF lending, and IMF gold sales would increase this exposure further by reducing the capital cushion of the IMF.
- Gold sales may deepen already serious moral hazard problems by leading to expectations by other distressed borrowers of further gold sales for debt relief. The volume of proposed gold sales already has expanded significantly in recent months.
- The proposal could help perpetuate and reinforce the IMF's drift toward becoming another development bank similar in many respects to the World Bank.
- The proposal may encourage the IMF to continue its policy of deeply subsidized interest rates, including the

IMF's reluctance to fully comply with the Congressional reforms mandated in 1998.
- The proposal has put downward pressure on gold prices and harmed poor nations that are also gold producers.

Joint Economic Committee
1537 Longworth House Office Building
Washington, DC 20515
Phone: 202-226-3234
Fax: 202-226-3950
Internet Address:
http://www.house.gov/jec/

CONTENTS

IMF gold sales in perspective 9

IMF Gold Holdings 11

Problems Posed by IMF Gold Sales 16

Lack of Transparency 16

Taxpayer Expense 19

IMF Loan Exposure 24

Gold Sales and Debt Relief 30

IMF Reform and Gold Sales 32

Market Disruptions 35

Conclusion 39

IMF GOLD SALES IN PERSPECTIVE

There have been a number of recent calls for the International Monetary Fund (IMF) to sell part of its 103 million ounce gold holdings as part of a debt relief plan for the heavily indebted poor countries (HIPC). One such proposal has been advanced by the Administration, and officials of several other nations as well as the IMF have voiced support for similar plans. The proposed gold sales would require Congressional approval, and debate on this change in policy is already underway.

Although the exact form of the proposal is not yet clear, there are several reasons for Congress to closely examine this proposal and review the potential negative consequences:

- The proposal is not transparent in that its content and full ramifications are unclear, and it may ultimately facilitate financing for certain IMF operations without conventional authorization and oversight.

- The proposed gold sales would tap a hidden IMF gold reserve that can be viewed as belonging to member countries. The cost of the proposal to the U.S. would amount to half a billion dollars, relative to restitution to member countries.

- Continued gold sales may weaken the IMF's balance sheet. With one-third of its outstanding credit from its main account owed by Russia and Indonesia, it is reasonable to question whether potential weakening of the IMF's financial position is desirable at this time. The money contributed by the taxpayers of the U.S. and other nations is exposed in IMF lending, and IMF gold sales would increase this exposure further by reducing the capital cushion of the IMF.

- Gold sales may deepen already serious moral hazard problems by leading to expectations by other distressed borrowers of further gold sales for debt relief. The volume of proposed gold sales already has expanded significantly in recent months.

- The proposal could help perpetuate and reinforce the IMF's drift toward becoming another development bank similar in many respects to the World Bank.

- The proposal may encourage the IMF to continue its policy of deeply subsidized interest rates; this would include the IMF's reluctance to fully comply with the

Congressional reforms mandated in 1998.
- The proposal has put downward pressure on gold prices and harmed poor nations that are also gold producers.

IMF Gold Holdings

The IMF holds 103 million ounces of gold originally acquired as quota contributions and through its transactions during the period when gold was a central element of the international monetary system. The collapse of the Bretton Woods system of fixed exchange rates in the early 1970's and subsequent policy decisions to demonetize gold were reflected in the second amendment to the IMF's Articles of Agreement in 1978. The second amendment officially demonetized gold and placed severe limitations on its use by the IMF or IMF member nations.

During the 1970s about one-third of the gold holdings of the IMF were disposed of in gold sales. The remaining gold was retained for a number of reasons, according to the IMF. These reasons include, "the potential unrealized gain on these assets may be considered a significant element adding to the overall strength of the IMF, that is, its basic—or ultimate—reserve;" in case of a "…need to meet creditors' claims on the institution in the event of liquidation..." and to provide resources if needed to "...encash members' reserve positions in the institution...;" and for "...unexpected systemic developments—that is, gold should be held as a reserve against future, unspecified contingencies...."[1]

Thus the gold reserve can be viewed as serving several purposes, including a provision for bad loans and a reserve against potential withdrawals of reserve positions by major donor nations. The potential use of gold as a reserve against donor withdrawals of reserves also reinforces the point made during Joint Economic Committee (JEC) hearings that padding or double counting of reserve accounts can be used as an accounting device to reduce the apparent level of usable resources available for IMF operations, thus justifying additional IMF appropriations. In any event, the IMF has identified a number of reasons to continue holding significant gold reserves.

On the other hand, the IMF identified several potential advantages to selling gold,

---

[1] Treasurer's Department (IMF), *Financial Organization and Operations of the IMF*, Washington, D.C., 1998, p.117.

including reduction of carrying and opportunity costs. In 1995 the IMF restated its policy on gold, recognizing that "any mobilization of gold should be carefully thought out to avoid any weakening in the IMF's overall financial position...."[2] and that "It must take great care to avoid causing disruption that would have an adverse impact on all gold holders and gold producers, as well as on the functioning of the gold market."[3] The IMF also maintained its position that "gold provides a fundamental strength to the IMF's balance sheet."[4]

In 1947 the IMF Executive Board asserted that the "gold and currency subscribed to the Fund are clearly within its unrestricted ownership. They do not belong in any way to the subscriber."[5] In the context of the Bretton Woods system and the official price of gold it established, this contention had an unambiguous meaning because the subscription price and the market value were essentially the same. However, the

---

2 *Ibid.*, p.117.

3 *Ibid.*, p.118.

4 *Ibid.*, p.117

5 Testimony of Harold J. Johnson, Jr., and Gary T. Engel, General Accounting Office, before the Joint Economic Committee, July 21, 1999, p.21.

breakdown of the system in the early 1970s created for the first time the possibility of a

large discrepancy between the official and the market price of gold. Only under these new circumstances could the value of the gold holdings increase significantly over their subscription value, and create the question of ownership of a surplus (capital gain). As we shall see, the IMF's restitution procedure renders this potentially troublesome legal issue largely irrelevant for the purposes of this analysis.

Perhaps in part due to the possibility of restitution to the member countries, the IMF values the gold on its financial statement at the old official price equivalent to about $48 per fine ounce, though its market value has been far higher since the mid-1970s. In light of potential restitution, this conservative accounting is quite defensible, but it does lead to potential issues in a broader policy context. For example, the value of the gold held in excess of $48 per ounce then becomes, in effect, a hidden reserve, and attempts to use this reserve for various policy objectives may have the effect of obscuring their costs to affected parties.

As noted, one of these policy objectives is to sell IMF gold to finance debt relief under the HIPC initiative. A review of this proposal brings to light several important problems. These problems include a lack of transparency, costs to the taxpayer, excessive IMF loan exposure, potential effects on IMF reform, and counterproductive effects on vulnerable poor countries. The balance of this paper will examine these issues in more detail.

Problems Posed by IMF Gold Sales

Lack of Transparency

According to recent GAO testimony before the Joint Economic Committee, [6]many of the details of the gold sales proposal are "non-public." Furthermore, in addition to its direct cost, the effects of the gold sales on IMF finances are very difficult to evaluate because of the obscurity of IMF financial statements which have proven confusing even to IMF officials in the past.

For example, as a lending institution, the IMF does not refer to its loans from its main lending account as "loans," but as "currency purchases." The central IMF budget is treated as a classified document, and separates usable from nonusable resources in IMF operations, a distinction that is not typically made in the public presentation of IMF financial accounts.

As noted, the details of the gold sales proposal, including even the amounts available for debt relief, are confidential. A complete and transparent analysis of the gold sales proposal on IMF finances is impossible

---

6 *Transparency and the Financial Structure of the IMF*, hearing of the Joint Economic Committee, July 21, 1999.

because this would require comparison of the confidential information of the gold sales proposal to data in a classified budget. This lack of transparency means that Congress is unable to make a fully informed decision on the gold sales proposal in consultation with independent experts and academics.

Although the available public information about the proposal is very inadequate, enough information can be assembled to show that the proposed gold sales raise funds by absorbing part of the hidden gold reserve not shown on the IMF's balance sheet.[7] These gold "profits" could then be invested in securities, and the interest generated used for debt relief. By tapping this hidden reserve, the proposal can be presented as a "free lunch" in that assets worth billions of dollars could be made available for IMF use without an apparent cost to anyone. However, at least from one point of view reflected in the IMF's own charter, most of the proceeds raised through the gold sales can be viewed as disguised contributions from major donor countries, though this fact is veiled inobscure IMF accounting and procedures.

---

7 A footnote to the IMF balance sheet does note the market value of gold holdings.

These concerns about IMF gold sales were recognized in 1975 in a joint bipartisan statement by Senator Ribicoff (D-Conn.) and Senator Taft (R-Ohio):

Either the gold belongs to the IMF, or it belongs to the member states, which contributed the gold in proportion to their quotas. **In either case, the profits should be distributed to the member nations in proportion to their quotas.**

The IMF is not designed to be a relief agency, nor an investment agency. If the nations owning stock in the International Bank for Reconstruction and Development [World Bank] wish to increase their subscriptions, or to increase their bilateral aid, out of IMF gold sale profits or with any other funds, then well and good. However, such a decision should be taken openly, by each nation, unencumbered by an artificial link between the question of aid and the role of gold in international payments.[8]

---

8 Comments of Senators Ribicoff and Taft, *The Proposed IMF Agreement on Gold*, Report of the Subcommittee on International Economics, Joint Economic Committee, December 17, 1975, p.11 (emphasis added).

Taxpayer Expense

As noted, IMF gold holdings reflect member contributions to, and transactions with, the IMF at a time when gold had a central role in the monetary system. After the collapse of the Bretton Woods system, gold was demonetized, but disagreements about the role of gold were reflected in a compromise amendment to the IMF charter in 1978 that severely limited the IMF's use of gold but permitted certain gold sales,[9] including what IMF documents refer to as "restitution." Dictionaries define restitution as "restoring to the rightful owner of something that has been taken away, lost, or surrendered." While significant restitution of IMF gold to members in the near term has not been proposed, restitution does provide a useful benchmark of the opportunity costs imposed by alternative proposals.

Under IMF rules, the IMF could restitute gold to member countries at a price currently equivalent to $48, according to a formula based on member contributions in 1975. Under this formula the U.S. would receive 23 percent of the amount of any gold restitution. For example, if 10 million ounces were restituted, the U.S. would receive 2.3 million

---

9 Treasurer's Department, *op. cit.,* pp.109-110

ounces. Under current market conditions, the U.S. would pay $110 million for this gold (2.3 million ounces multiplied by $48 per ounce), but then receive an asset worth $592 million, leading to a total net gain of $482 million.[10] Restitution is a useful benchmark to use in evaluating other forms of gold sales in terms of potential costs to the taxpayers of the U.S. and other affected nations.

As noted, the gold held by the IMF is valued on the IMF balance sheet at equivalent to $48 per fine ounce, relative to a current market price of about $257. The undervalued IMF book value of gold creates a hidden IMF gold reserve of over $21 billion (see graph below). The recent IMF gold sales proposal would tap part of this hidden reserve to finance the debt restructuring plan. If 10 million ounces of gold were sold for about $2.6 billion at current market prices, about $2.1 billion of the total would be generated by the value of gold not shown on the balance sheet. This is the hidden cost to donor countries in terms

---

[10] Assuming a price of $48 per fine ounce for 2.3 million ounces would generate $110.4 million in revenue to the IMF. The 2.3 million ounces of gold held by the U.S. would be worth $592 million, resulting in a net profit of $482 million. This is based on a market price of $257.30 per fine ounce as of August 4, 1999.

IMF GOLD SALES IN PERSPECTIVE

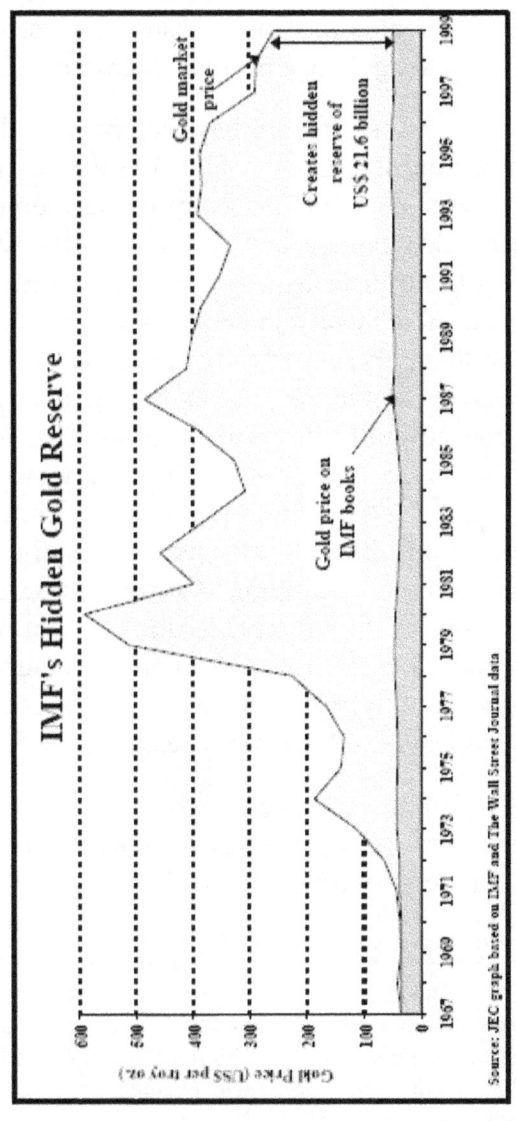

of foregone profits. The effect would be the same if some other mechanism were used to tap into the gold reserve to finance debt relief.

Though the proposal has been presented as something of a "free lunch" by its sponsors, the hidden or obscured nature of its costs do not make them nonexistent. By tapping the value of gold not appearing on the IMF's balance sheet, these costs can be obscured, but once identified, these costs are quite significant. Relative to the restitution benchmark, the proposed gold sales will cost the U.S. and its taxpayers $482 million. For every billion dollars of IMF gold sales not in the form of restitution, the U.S. cost is $187 million.[11] Furthermore, in addition to the proceeds from the gold value not on the balance sheet, the capital value of the gold, or $48 per ounce, goes directly to the main IMF account, the General Resources Account (GRA).

Potential taxpayer expense is an important issue especially in light of the highly concentrated financing of the IMF

---

11   This figure is derived from the United States' share of $230 million (or 894,000 ounces) out of total restitution amounting to $1 billion. This $230 million of gold minus $43 million in payments to the IMF leaves a net value of $187 million.

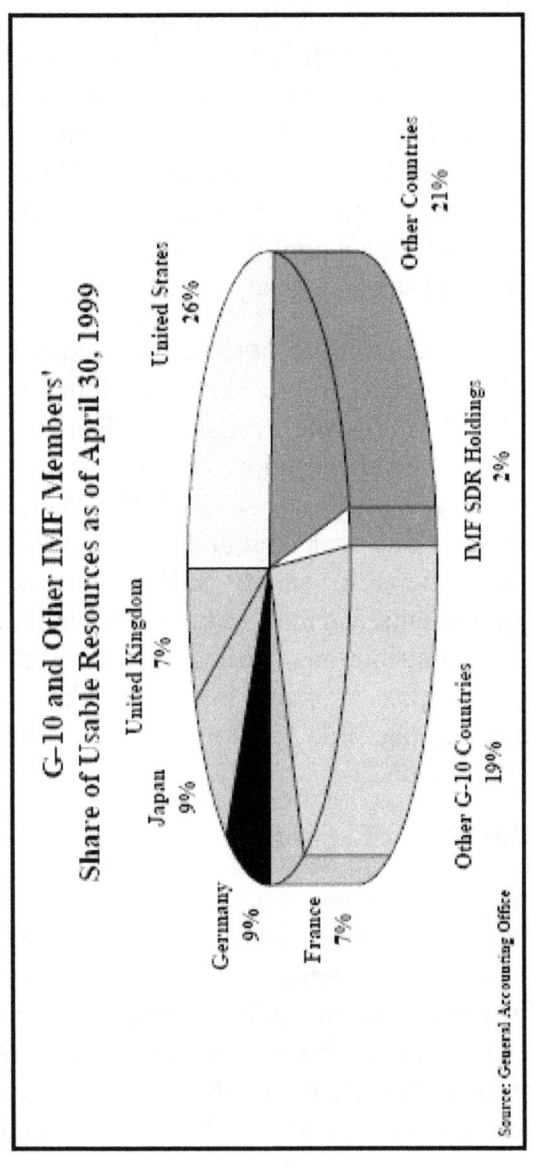

G-10 and Other IMF Members'
Share of Usable Resources as of April 30, 1999

United States 26%
Other Countries 21%
IMF SDR Holdings 2%
Other G-10 Countries 19%
France 7%
Germany 9%
Japan 9%
United Kingdom 7%

Source: General Accounting Office

as a whole. The U.S. already provides 26 percent of the IMF's $195 billion of usable contributions; the G-10 countries as a whole provide 77 percent of the usable resources for IMF operations (see graph below). Many of these same nations will again make another disproportionate contribution if the proposed IMF gold sales were approved.

It is interesting to note that the remaining 171 members of the IMF contribute only 21% of its usable resources. Nearly half of IMF member nations maintain little or no reserve positions at the IMF. Many of these nations make required hard currency contributions to satisfy IMF membership requirements, and then immediately withdraw these contributions without affecting their voting rights. In short, the voting shares of countries has little relation to their financial participation.

IMF Loan Exposure

As an "ultimate reserve," IMF gold sales must be viewed in the context of the IMF's finances and lending policies. The lack of diversification in IMF lending, including a heavy concentration in certain countries that are questionable credit risks, is not very well known. As of April 30, 1999, about

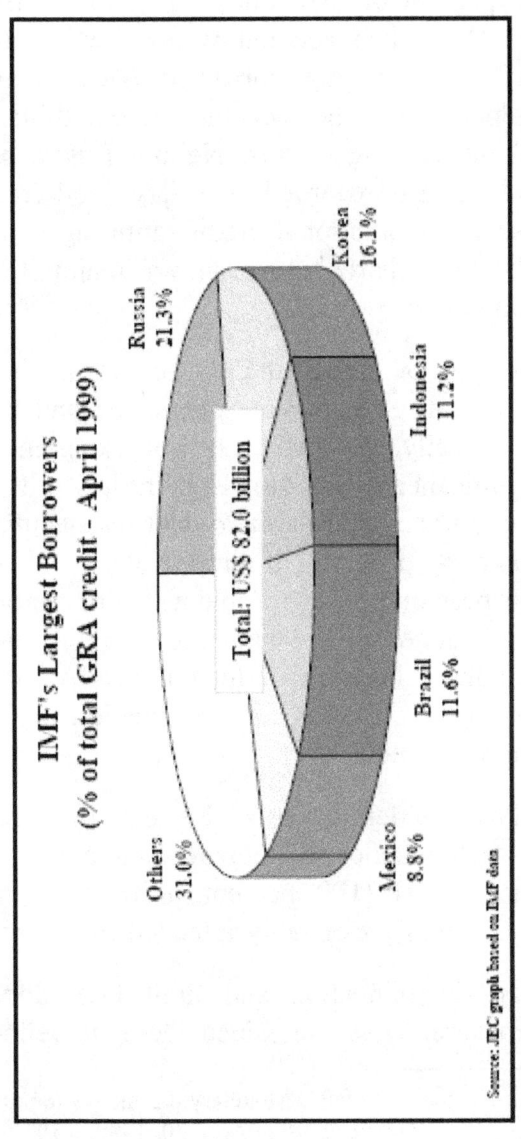

70 percent of IMF outstanding loans from the IMF main account were owed by the IMF's five largest borrowers.[12] Russia and Indonesia together account for one-third of all outstanding credits. Neither Russia nor Indonesia is regarded as a very good credit risk by international credit rating agencies. The pie chart below shows major IMF borrowers:

It may be argued that any concerns about IMF loan exposure are overstated and that historically the IMF has not experienced significant defaults. However, the lack of IMF transparency and *de facto* debt rescheduling make it difficult to empirically evaluate the past or present problems. Furthermore, the changes in the nature of IMF lending and the relaxation of loan limits have led to a very different current situation that is unprecedented.

Past guidelines used by the IMF had restricted the level of borrowing to a nation's quota level (100 percent of quota). This policy was presumably intended to promote

loan diversification and limit IMF donor exposure. However, since these guidelines

---

[12] International Monetary Fund *Financial Statements*, Quarter Ending April 30, 1999, p.10.

were relaxed, IMF loans may rise as high as several hundred percent of a borrower's quota contribution (around 500 percent in the case of Korea). Over its entire history, it is doubtful that the IMF has ever had such a sizeable proportion of its outstanding credit owed by such large and dubious credit risks, at least one of which has had to borrow from the IMF for the purpose of servicing its IMF loan. Thus, it is reasonable to question whether further erosion in the financial position of the IMF is desirable at this time by liquidation of reserves that could help cover potential loan losses and help create the confidence of its ability to do so.

Underlying the concentration of IMF lending to dubious credit risks is a major change in the nature of IMF lending. Over the last few decades, the IMF has transformed itself from a lender for balance of payments purposes to a longer-term lender for development and economic restructuring. This transformation reflects the collapse of the Bretton Woods system and the search for a new mission to justify IMF activities, but it also entails potentially greater risks. Recent IMF borrowers have broader and deeper systematic problems than the kind of balance of payments pressures financed by the IMF in the previous era. This evolution entails the potential for higher risk from longer loan maturity, type and use of loans, and the credit risk of borrowers. The graph below documents the trend in IMF lending since the collapse of the Bretton Woods arrangement.

The drift of the IMF towards becoming another development lender similar to the World Bank raises a number of important policy issues regarding the IMF's finances. The fact that IMF gold holdings could act as a loan loss reserve suggests that the greater risks of recent IMF lending should be balanced by retention of the gold reserve, at least for the foreseeable future.

Furthermore, given the changing view of gold by official institutions, the current proposal can be seen as a precedent for similar IMF gold sales in the future. This could lead to further pressures to erode more of the gold reserve in a way that is not in the interest of the taxpayers of donor countries.

The proposed gold sales would also enhance moral hazard in several ways. The perception that gold sales are something of a "free lunch" may ultimately encourage

IMF GOLD SALES IN PERSPECTIVE

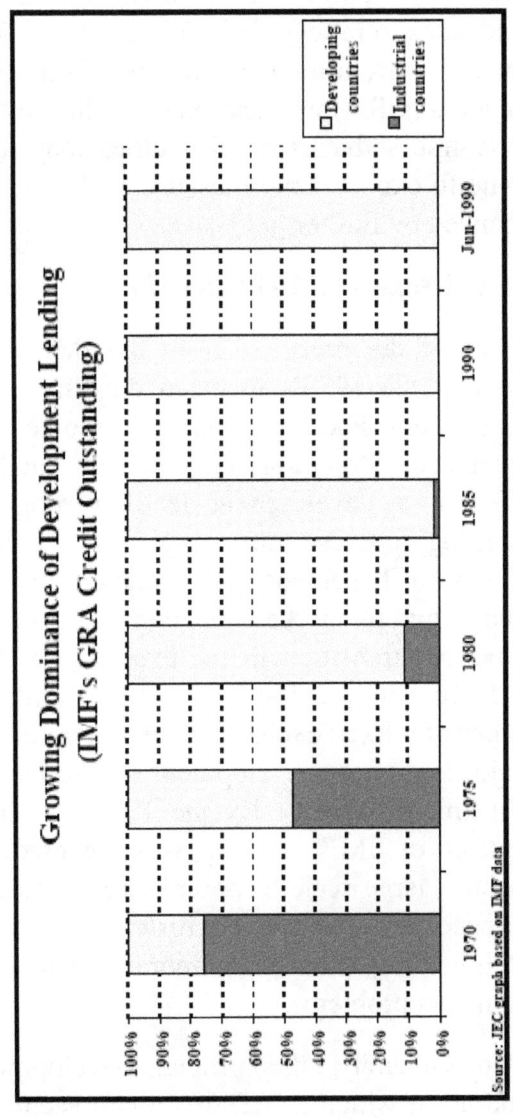

other IMF borrowers to favor or expect gold sales to relieve their debt burdens. IMF borrowers from the main General Resources Account (GRA) who are experiencing severe economic setbacks or difficulties may also come to expect some measure of debt relief financed by further gold sales.

Gold Sales and Debt Relief

Part of the proceeds from the IMF gold sales of the 1970's financed the Structural Adjustment Facility, later to become the Enhanced Structural Adjustment Facility (ESAF), a development lending program charging interest rates typically as low as 0.5 to 1 percent. The creation of this loan program marked the beginning of an important transition in the evolution of the IMF from its previous monetary role at the center of a fixed exchange rate system into a major lender for development and structural adjustment projects. By the 1990s, a large portion of IMF lending was devoted to various large-scale economic restructuring purposes, which were very different in nature from lending to bridge temporary balance of payments problems.

Unfortunately, the official development lending of which ESAF was a part seems to have become more of a hindrance than a help to many of the poor borrowing countries. The IMF recognizes that the total debt burden of many countries is larger than many of these borrowers are willing or able to service, and so the IMF has agreed to assist in financing the HIPC initiative. To help do so, the IMF would seek contributions from members and if these did not suffice, the IMF would attempt to win approval for gold sales. However, this juncture also provides an opportunity to reevaluate this IMF-sponsored activity and whether it should be continued.

Given the current controversy over debt relief, it is reasonable to question whether it is necessary or desirable for the IMF to sponsor something like ESAF, a lending program more appropriately conducted by the World Bank. ESAF has become part of the official debt burdening underdeveloped countries, and it appears that the proceeds from gold sales could be used to help maintain its operations for the next several years. If ESAF were terminated, over $2 billion in ESAF reserves might be made available for other purposes, including debt relief. The termination of ESAF would be a desirable first step in refocusing the IMF on short-term crisis lending and away from a continued evolution into another development bank.

Alternatively, the implementation of the gold sales proposal would help gloss-over the failures of the development strategies fostered by the official institutions. This proposal would also continue, if not reinforce, the IMF's current drift into development and structural lending, not only in ESAF but in the lending from the General Resources Account (GRA) of the IMF as well. An alternative policy approach would be to terminate ESAF as an activity more appropriately conducted by the World Bank than by the IMF. ESAF reserves might be made available for debt restructuring and relief.

IMF Reform and Gold Sales

The IMF makes loans that are all heavily subsidized in varying degrees by the use of below market interest rates. For example, the standard IMF loan rate, currently about 3.8 percent, is considerably below the standard international reference rates such as LIBOR (London Interbank Offered Rate). The IMF's alternative premium rate for circumstances typical in bailout situations is currently about 6.8 percent.

The IMF's subsidized interest rates were one focus of the debate over the 1998 IMF appropriation in Congress. These interest rate subsidies became an issue because they distort price signals, are economically inefficient, and deepen already pervasive moral hazard problems. Much of the debate on these issues was stimulated by the *IMF Transparency and Efficiency Act*, a reform measure that provided for the use of market interest rates on all IMF loans. At the final stage of the legislative process, JEC staff was asked to assist in drafting reform language regarding IMF interest rates on loans used in typical crisis situations. This language, a version of which finally became law, stipulates that IMF interest rates under these crisis circumstances must be adjusted for risk. A formula for a minimum interest rate was provided for the sole purpose of preventing excessive discretion, and not for pegging the interest rate.

However, it remains unclear whether the IMF recognizes that the reform legislation requires an adjustment for risk, and does not replicate existing IMF interest rate formulae. In any event, as an alternative method of financing the IMF's HIPC contribution, the IMF could use a true adjustment for risk on affected loans, and thus generate higher interest earnings for debt relief. These premium interest rates would no longer be as deeply subsidized, and could provide the approximately $100 million annually for debt relief that is called for. Another option would be to slightly increase the deeply subsidized standard IMF loan interest rate.

It is to be expected that the IMF will resist such suggestions to reduce interest rate subsidies. Exorbitant interest subsidies are central to IMF's current operations. Additionally, the IMF would presumably argue that it is not desirable to use interest earnings from the main IMF account and channel part of it to ESAF for debt relief. However, the gold and certain interest, both already associated with the GRA, have been considered as sources of funding for debt relief, and an argument that only some proceeds arising from the GRA can be tapped but not others is not very persuasive. Furthermore, it appears likely that the funds raised by the gold sales would ultimately end up in the GRA.

A very small rise in IMF interest rates could easily cover the costs of the debt relief initiative, as could the $2 billion in reserves already in the ESAF. However, these options would require the IMF to modestly reform its practices or use its own resources, but neither of these choices seems to have been seriously considered. Instead, a veiled way of tapping more resources by the IMF at taxpayer expense through gold sales has been the preferred course.

Market Disruptions

For an agency that presents itself as a stabilizing force in international markets, the effects of the IMF's proposed gold sales have been especially ironic. In the wake of clear signals from central banks, especially the Bank of England, that the status of gold was changing and that market sales were looming, the IMF and other proponents persisted in the proposal for additional market sales. While sorting out the precise impact of this proposal and its endorsement by the G-7 finance ministries is not possible, there is a widespread view that the IMF proposal has been a negative force in the gold markets (see graph below). After the IMF proposal was finalized, gold market prices drifted below the costs of production in at least one key producer country.

As the IMF Treasurer's Department itself pointed out only last year:

An important element in considering potential gold sales by the IMF is that such sales -- or even the announcement of an intent to sell -- could, at least in the short run, cause the market price of gold to fall. Various official holders of gold that value their stock at or in relation to the market price may view with concern a sharp decline in the value of their holdings because of an announced program of gold sales by the IMF.[13]

---

13 Treasurer's Department (IMF), *op. cit.*, p.117.

IMF GOLD SALES IN PERSPECTIVE

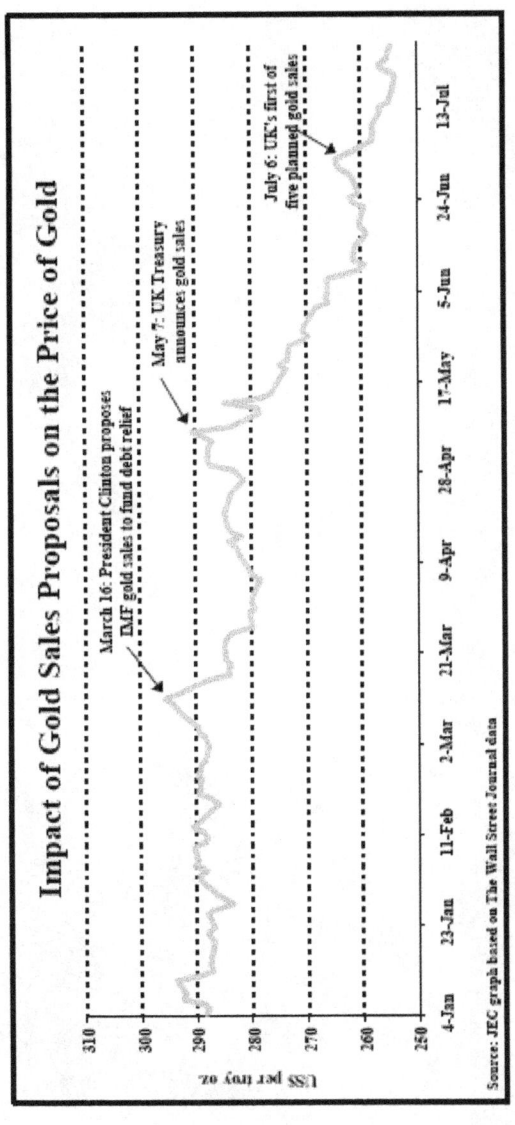

Conclusion

Proposals for use of taxpayer resources by the IMF should be fully explained in a transparent manner. The failure of the IMF and Administration to provide details on the proposed gold sales to Congress and the public does not permit fully informed consideration of this policy and possible alternatives. A complete explanation of this or any similar proposal should be provided to Congress and the public by the IMF or the Treasury. The costs of the proposal, and all costs associated with the IMF, should also routinely be delineated and provided to Congress, instead of the official pronouncements that there are no taxpayer costs associated with participation in the IMF.

Congressional concerns about lack of IMF transparency and IMF interest rate subsidies are reflected in enacted reforms that have become law. Approval of the proposed IMF gold sales could have the effect of delaying needed IMF reforms and be viewed as sanctioning IMF loan subsidies and current development policy under the IMF and ESAF. On the other hand, rejection of the proposed gold sales would send a strong message to the IMF that its current policies of loan subsidization and development lending lack support in Congress, and that genuine IMF reform is required.

Christopher Frenze
Chief Economist to the Vice Chairman

Alexandre Ferraz de Marinis provided research assistance for this study.

Notes

Notes

Notes

NOTES

www.ingramcontent.com/pod-product-compliance
Lightning Source LLC
LaVergne TN
LVHW041501070426
835507LV00009B/741